Find your way with words

Types *of* Words

Rebecca Vickers

Heinemann
LIBRARY

Chicago, Illinois

© 2013 Heinemann Library
an imprint of Capstone Global Library, LLC
Chicago, Illinois

To contact Capstone Global Library, please
call 800-747-4992, or visit our web site,
www.capstonepub.com

Edited by Andrew Farrow, Laura Hensley,
Vaarunika Dharmapala, Helen Cox Cannons
Designed by Philippa Jenkins
Original illustrations © Capstone Global Library
Ltd
Illustrated by Capstone Global Library Ltd
Picture research by Tracy Cummins
Production by Sophia Argyris
Printed in China by Leo Paper Products Ltd

17 16 15 14 13
10 9 8 7 6 5 4 3 2 1

**Library of Congress Cataloging-in-Publication
Data**
Vickers, Rebecca.
  Types of Words : Unleashing Powerful Parts of
Speech / Rebecca Vickers.
     pages cm.—(Find your way with words)
  Includes bibliographical references and index.
  ISBN 978-1-4329-7657-6 (hb)—ISBN 978-1-4329-
7662-0 (pb) 1. English language—Parts of speech.
2. English language—Grammar. I. Title.

PE1112.V55 2014
425—dc23   2012039621

Acknowledgments
Alamy p. 44 right (© GL Archive); Getty Images
pp. 5 (Robert Abbott Sengstacke/Contributor), 13
(Diana Hirsch), 15 (Dorling Kindersley), 23
(Buyenlarge/Contributor), 27 (W. & D. Downey),
45 (Keystone-France/Gamma-Keystone); Library
of Congress Prints and Photographs pp. 37, 44 left;
Picture Desk p. 10 (NEW LINE / SAUL ZAENTZ /
WING NUT / THE KOBAL COLLECTION),
Punchstock p. 33 (Brand X Photos); Shutterstock
pp. 4 (© Darko Zeljkovic), 7 (© Monkey Business
Images), 8 (© meunierd), 9 (© Photobac), 16
(© wrangler), 19 (© Yuri Arcurs), 20 (© shock),
21 (© Mayskyphoto), 25 (© TonyV3112), 29
(© Stefan Schurr), 31 (© SF photo), 34 (© Keith
Gentry), 35 (© Mircea BEZERGHEANU), 36
(© bikeriderlondon), 38 (© Alan Mardi), 39
(© Anastasiia Markus), 40 (© Vitalii Nesterchuk),
42 (© HitToon.Com), 43 (© Vertes Edmond Mihai),
47 phone (© bloomua), 47 swimmer (© Schmid
Christophe).

Back cover photograph of three athletes made
of modeling clay reproduced by Shutterstock
(© Alan Mardi).

We would like to thank Joanna John for her
invaluable help in the preparation of this book.

Contents

Let's Be Clear

Language is all about communication. How you speak, talk, or write to different people in different situations will depend on how you use language. Whether you write a political speech, school essay, or tweet or make a phone call, communicating clearly and using the best words in the right order is the key to being understood.

Grammar is the structure of a language

English, like all languages, has a special structure with rules that determine its shape. This is called grammar. The rules of English grammar have developed over hundreds of years and continue to change. In the same way that computer code formats the way a computer works and gives it the ability to function, grammar gives a meaningful shape to groups of words. This formatting of words into a recognized and accepted order is called syntax.

Why does it matter?

Here are a few reasons why it makes sense to learn the rules and structure of grammar:

- Clarity: When you learn to speak and write effectively, your words are more easily understood. You can always say or write exactly what you mean without risk of confusion. This is particularly important when you are giving instructions or reporting a real event.
- Language and thought: Thinking clearly and writing clearly are linked. If your arguments are not clearly thought out, this often shows up in your grammar. In the worlds of education and work, being interesting, precise, and clear can give you an advantage.
- Mental representation: The way our brains store language reflects grammatical structures. Even if you think you do not know anything about grammar, your mind still retains language in this way. If your language does not reflect this, you will find it hard to be understood by others.

Even tweets sent via cell phones or computers have to follow rules— a tweet can only be 140 characters long.

Some speakers, such as Dr. Martin Luther King, Jr. (1929–1968), are remembered for the quality and moving content of their speeches. Using the right language choices can make a speaker's words unforgettable. Dr. King's words, like these below, were always well chosen and used images and ideas people find easy to understand:

> *Let us not seek to satisfy our thirst for freedom by drinking from the cup of bitterness and hatred.*

WORDS IN ACTION

Using words well

Powerful, accurate, and interesting writing uses many types of words. It makes you want to read more. This passage from *The Hunger Games,* by American author Suzanne Collins (born 1962), uses many of the types of words this book covers:

> As soon as I am in the trees, I retrieve a bow and sheath of arrows from a hollow log. Electrified or not, the fence has been successful at keeping the flesh-eaters out of District 12. Inside the woods they roam freely, and there are added concerns like venomous snakes, and no real paths to follow.

From *The Hunger Games* by Suzanne Collins, published by Scholastic Inc. in 2008

Understanding Word Types

The words used in a language perform different functions. Some give names to objects or people, while others describe actions. In English, these word groups are called parts of speech. Most language experts divide English into eight, nine, or ten different parts of speech. In this book, nine different parts of speech will be explored. Each of these groups of words has a name and its own function, or use.

Word type	Simple definition	Some examples
Noun	Word that names a person, place, thing, feeling, quality, or idea	woman, mountain, road, anger, height, freedom
Pronoun	Word that is used in place of a noun	you, me, hers, who, these, everyone, himself
Adjective	Word used to describe a noun or pronoun	small, blue, eight, thrilling, smoky
Verb	Word that says what a noun or a pronoun does or what it is	go, drink, is, seem, demonstrate
Adverb	Word that describes or modifies a verb or another adverb	inside, slowly, later, too slow, impossibly
Preposition	Word that shows the relationship between a noun or pronoun and other words in a sentence	above, from, with
Determiner	Word that limits or modifies a noun	the, some, both
Conjunction	Word that joins other words, phrases, or sentences	and, but, or
Interjection	Word used, usually on its own with an exclamation mark, to express an emotion or surprise	Ouch! Help! Bang!

Subject and predicate:
Something or someone doing something

In both written and spoken language, the parts of speech are organized into sentences. Every sentence must contain a noun and a verb in order to be complete. The noun and any words that relate to it are called the subject of the sentence. The verb and other words that relate to it are known as the predicate of the sentence. In the sentence The cat sat on the mat, the subject is The cat and the predicate is sat on the mat. Keeping the words that relate to each other together helps make the meaning clear.

QUICK TIP

Is it 8, 9, or 10?

Why do different sources give different numbers of parts of speech? There are eight traditional parts of speech (noun, verb, adjective, adverb, preposition, pronoun, conjunction, and interjection). However, some experts divide verbs into two different types—main verbs and auxiliary verbs— which makes nine total parts of speech. Other people class determiners (including articles) as a separate part of speech, rather than as adjectives. In this book, we will look at nine types of words: the eight traditional parts of speech, plus determiners.

Every word you speak, write down, or read is a part of speech.

Whether they are objects, people, or places, all of the things in the universe have names. The words used to name things are called nouns. Our names, and the names of our friends, pets, and the towns we live in, are proper nouns (see page 10). In order to be complete, every sentence must include a noun as its subject.

Common nouns

The words used for everyday objects, people, animals, and places are known as common nouns. Examples of common nouns include man, ship, horse, flower, pen, hospital, river, and town. A common noun does not start with a capital letter, unless it is at the beginning of a sentence.

This big cat [common noun] is a Bengal tiger [precise noun] in an enclosure [common noun] at the zoo [common noun] in Berlin [proper noun].

Precise nouns

Many common nouns are very general. Words such as dog, flower, and rock could mean anything in that category. To be more specific, a precise noun is needed—for example, terrier instead of dog, rose instead of flower, and quartz instead of rock. A precise noun gives more detail to the reader or listener.

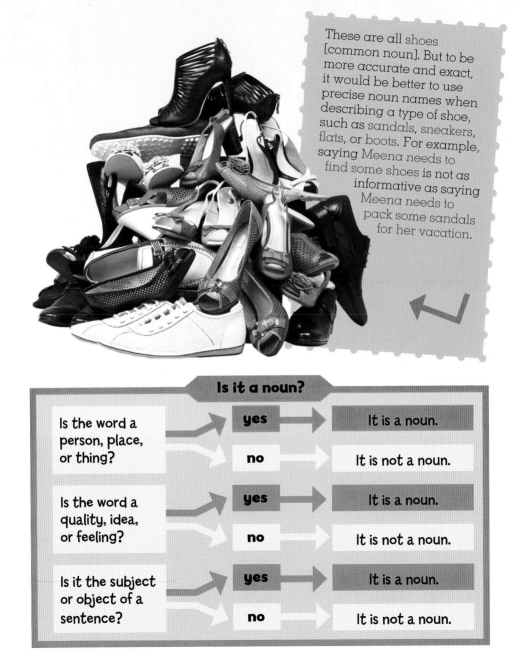

These are all shoes [common noun]. But to be more accurate and exact, it would be better to use precise noun names when describing a type of shoe, such as sandals, sneakers, flats, or boots. For example, saying Meena needs to find some shoes is not as informative as saying Meena needs to pack some sandals for her vacation.

Is it a noun?

Is the word a person, place, or thing?	yes	It is a noun.
	no	It is not a noun.
Is the word a quality, idea, or feeling?	yes	It is a noun.
	no	It is not a noun.
Is it the subject or object of a sentence?	yes	It is a noun.
	no	It is not a noun.

Proper nouns

When a word is the name of a specific person, place, or thing, then it is known as a proper noun. Every person's given name is a proper noun—Jake, Maria, Emma, Jackson, Alex, and so on. The individual names given to pets, racehorses, ships, and buildings are all proper nouns. All geographic names for places are proper nouns, such as Atlantic Ocean, New York, Atlas Mountains, and Gobi Desert. The words in proper nouns always start with a capital letter.

WORDS IN ACTION

Made-up people and places

Fiction authors sometimes create entire countries or worlds filled with rulers and inhabitants. Hogwarts School of Witchcraft and Wizardry in the *Harry Potter* books by J. K. Rowling (born 1965) is an imaginary place, but the names of all its locations and inhabitants are still proper nouns:

> At the end nearest him sat Hagrid, who caught his eye and gave the thumbs-up. Harry grinned back. And there, in the center of the High Table, in a large gold chair, sat Albus Dumbledore. Harry recognized him at once from the card he'd got out of the Chocolate Frog on the train...Harry spotted Professor Quirrell, too, the nervous young man from the Leaky Cauldron.

From *Harry Potter and the Philosopher's Stone* by J. K. Rowling.
Copyright © J.K. Rowling

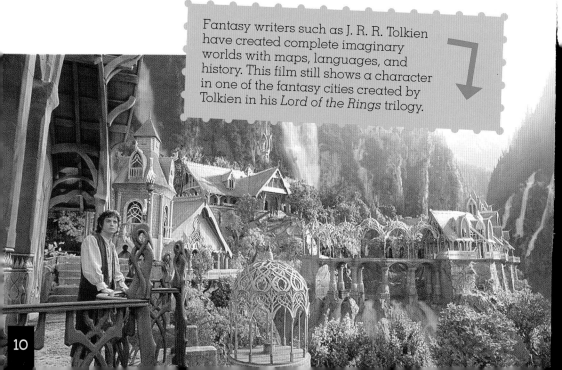

Fantasy writers such as J. R. R. Tolkien have created complete imaginary worlds with maps, languages, and history. This film still shows a character in one of the fantasy cities created by Tolkien in his *Lord of the Rings* trilogy.

Compound nouns

Sometimes nouns are joined together to make another word. For example, when you join together soccer and shoe to make soccer shoe, you have a different word with a different meaning. When the words boy and friend are joined together into boyfriend, the word means something more. These words are called compound words.

Number: Plurals and collective nouns

Number is the word used in grammar to say whether one thing is meant or if more than one is meant. In number for nouns, the term singular means one thing and the word plural means more than one. Usually a noun is made plural by adding an -s. Here are some tricky ones that don't follow the rule:

- Sometimes the plural of a noun is a different word. For example, woman is the singular form, and women is the plural form of the same word.
- Singular nouns that end in -ch, -s, -sh, -x, and -z add -es to become plural—for example, singular church becomes plural churches.
- Singular nouns that end in a -y that follows a consonant drop the y and add -ies to become plural, such as butterfly to butterflies. If the letter before the y is a vowel, then the y stays and an -s is added, such as day to days.
- Usually nouns that end in -o when singular add -es if the o comes after a consonant, such as potato to potatoes. When the o comes after a vowel, only an -s is added, such as cuckoo to cuckoos.
- When a singular form of a noun ends in -f or -fe, usually the plural form drops the f or fe and adds -ves, such as thief to thieves and wife to wives.

Remember that, with all these exceptions to the rule, there will be more exceptions! So, when in doubt, always check in a dictionary.

Collective nouns are nouns that describe a group of individuals in the singular. For example, words like family or committee cover a number of people, but they describe one single family or committee. You would say The family has decided to go to Disney World for a vacation, using the word has instead of have, even though you are talking about many people. Collective nouns can also be made plural in the normal way if there is more than one of them: a committee becomes two or more committees.

Count and noncount nouns

When a noun is made plural, it is just a matter of a changed ending, usually an s. These are nouns that are called count nouns because they can be counted—one dog, two dogs, and so on. But some words are exceptions to this rule. They are noncount or mass nouns. They represent nouns that cannot be counted. Think about words such as rice, sand, and wheat. They cannot be counted in the traditional way. Be careful not to make these words plural by adding an s.

Abstract nouns: Ideas, qualities, and feelings

Sometimes the "thing" that is the subject of a sentence is not something you can touch or see. It might be a feeling, idea, or quality. This kind of word is called an abstract noun. An abstract noun can be used as the subject of a sentence, just like a common noun. Here are some examples:

The happiness [abstract noun] of the athlete makes her play better.
Freedom [abstract noun] is what all enslaved people hope for.
The poverty [abstract noun] in Haiti makes rebuilding more difficult.

Nouns and gender

In some languages, all nouns have a gender—the words themselves are considered masculine (male) or feminine (female). This means that they often have to be used with other words of the same gender. For example, in French the word cat (chat) is considered masculine, even if the cat being discussed is a female cat. The word is a masculine word. However, in English, the only words that have gender are those used to represent someone who actually is male or female:
• Some male nouns: boy, son, father, James, stallion, and bull
• Some female nouns: girl, daughter, mother, Megan, mare, and cow.

There are also nouns that have no gender or can represent either sex:
• No gender: flower, chair, wind
• Common gender: cousin, parent, sibling.

Other nouns can be changed from representing male or female to the other gender, by changing the word ending or by adding another or different word:
• Changing the word ending: actor (male) to actress (female), hero (male) to heroine (female)
• Adding a different word: landlord (male) to landlady (female), bride (female) to bridegroom (male).

In English, the only way in which nouns need to agree with another word of the same gender is nouns with pronouns (see pages 16–17). For example, if you are talking about a bride, you would need to use female pronouns such as her and she: The **bride** wore **her** white high heels all day, even though **she** found them uncomfortable.

This image shows the heroine [female] and hero [male] from a story. These words are different and depend on the gender of the character. The pronouns must agree with the gender of the character as well—so she and her with heroine, and he and him with hero.

When a noun is the object of the action

In addition to being the subject of a sentence, a noun can also receive the action in a sentence: Nick [subject] threw [predicate] the ball [object]. When this happens, the noun becomes the object of the sentence. If the action of the verb used is directed at the object, it is known as a direct object: Milly ironed **the skirt**. There can also be nouns that are indirect objects in a sentence. An indirect object lets us know to whom, or for what, the action in the verb is performed. Here is an example: **The actor** [subject] showed **the director** [indirect object] his **audition speech** [direct object].

Choose the right noun

When you write or speak, choosing the correct noun can make all the difference. Remember the following three points to help you make the right choice:

1. Always be exact if it is important to what you are saying. This is what precise nouns and proper nouns are for. If you are making a poster to help you find your lost dog, it would be clearer and more helpful to mention that the dog's breed is cocker spaniel, rather than just saying lost dog, and to say that the dog's proper name is Rosie.

2. Don't forget to use abstract nouns, especially if you are being creative. These nouns can add depth and emotion to writing and speech. Here is the first verse of a poem by the American poet Emily Dickinson (1830–1886), which describes the abstract noun hope:

   > "Hope" is the thing with feathers–
   > That perches in the soul–
   > And sings the tune without the words–
   > And never stops–at all–

3. Make sure that whatever noun you choose is the right gender and number. If it is a plural or a collective noun, make sure it agrees with all the other words in the sentence (see page 11).

QUICK TIP

Grab that dictionary!

The best reference source to help you find out about any word is a dictionary. These guides list words in alphabetical order and explain the spelling, type, meaning, and history of words. Dictionaries can be found as books, online, or as apps. See page 48 for a full explanation of how to get the most out of a dictionary entry.

Your name is a proper noun!

All of our first names and last names are proper nouns. Parents usually choose the first names of their children based on personal preference or cultural or family tradition. Over the past 500 years, last names have been adopted and passed from generation to generation.

Most last names developed from professions, descriptions, nicknames, place names, or family relationships. This blacksmith could have passed down the name "Smith" to his descendants because of his job; or he could have passed down "Black" because of his hair color; or "Hill" for where he lived; or "Jackson," showing his relationship to his father, Jack.

Pronouns are words that are used in place of a noun: **She** [pronoun] loves wearing **her** [pronoun] red **jeans** [common noun]. Pronouns are very useful in writing and speaking because they can keep you from having to repeat nouns. A pronoun does not give you the same information as a noun, since it does not name the noun.

QUICK TIP

Nouns needed

When you use pronouns in speaking and in writing, always make sure that it is absolutely clear what nouns the pronouns are replacing. For example, if you say She loves the feeling of sand between her toes, it is not clear who the "she" is. If you first said Ayeesha is going to the beach, then it is clear who it is that the pronouns "she" and "her" are replacing.

I think you and she should come with me. Then, they could go with her.

If too many pronouns are used or repeated without it being clear who is being referred to, it can be very confusing!

Pronoun types

There are many types of pronoun. See the chart on page 49 for a full list. Each pronoun type is used in a different way to replace a noun:

- Personal pronouns: Personal pronouns represent the speaker, the one being spoken to, or the people, places, or things being referred to. I, you, it, my, your, and their are all personal pronouns.

- Demonstrative pronouns: Demonstrative pronouns are used to stand for a specific thing or things. They point out or bring attention to something. This, that, those, and these are the demonstrative pronouns: **These** are her favorite shoes.

- Possessive pronouns: Possessive pronouns show possession of something. They include mine, yours, hers, his, and ours: **Yours** isn't finished yet, but **mine** is ready.

- Relative pronouns: The relative pronouns are who, whom, whose, which, and that. They are called relative pronouns because they relate one word or a group of words to others. Here is an example: The boy **who** broke the window is in my class. In this sentence, who relates to boy, and it introduces the information **who** broke the window, known as a relative clause.

- Interrogative pronouns: Interrogative pronouns are used to ask questions. They represent the things that are the focus of the questions being asked. The four main interrogative pronouns are what, which, who, and whom. For example: **Who** will go with me to see the teacher?

- Reciprocal pronouns: In a sentence where two or more people are doing or feeling the same thing, reciprocal pronouns may be used. The two reciprocal pronouns are each other and one another. Here is an example: Dogs and cats hate **each other**.

- Indefinite pronouns: Indefinite pronouns do not represent any specific person, place, thing, or amount. They are general and nonspecific and include all, any, everyone, many, one, and some. For example: **Everyone** thinks the player cheated.

- Reflexive pronouns: Reflexive pronouns are used when there is a need to refer back to the subject of a sentence. There are five singular reflexive pronouns: myself, yourself, himself, herself, and itself. There are three plural reflexive pronouns: ourselves, yourselves, and themselves. Here is an example: They cannot help **themselves**. Reflexive pronouns are called intensive reflexive pronouns when used with another pronoun for extra emphasis: I **myself** found the exam very difficult.

- Numerical pronouns: Numbers, such as cardinal numbers (one, two, three) and ordinal numbers (first, second, third), can be used as pronouns: **One** of the team members suffered a bad injury. He was the **third** this season.

Not a pronoun, an adjective!

Many words can be used in more than one way. Depending on how they are used, they become a different part of speech. Words that are indefinite pronouns are also sometimes used as adjectives (see pages 20–23). For example, in the sentence Do you have **another**?, another is used as an indefinite pronoun. However, in this sentence, Do you have **another** dress without buttons?, another is being used as an adjective.

QUICK TIP

Pronouns all on their own

You can use some pronouns that don't substitute for a noun without getting it wrong! When speaking or writing in the first person, I doesn't need a prior noun: I love that dress. If you are referring to someone using the personal pronoun you, both people involved know who is meant: You handled that problem really well. If a question is being asked, the pronoun being used doesn't need to be replacing a noun: Who just came in? or What did you have for dinner? The pronoun it can also be used in some circumstances without replacing a noun: It is time to leave.

WORDS IN ACTION

Using the first person

In the novel *A Fast and Brutal Wing* by American author Kathleen Jeffrie Johnson, different chapters contain the first person viewpoints of different characters. Here is an excerpt:

Sometimes I pass the old house where that crazy writer lives. Every so often I see him watching me, but I just blend back into the trees until I'm alone.

From *A Fast and Brutal Wing*, published by Roaring Brook Press in 2004

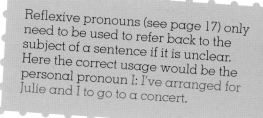

Reflexive pronouns (see page 17) only need to be used to refer back to the subject of a sentence if it is unclear. Here the correct usage would be the personal pronoun I: I've arranged for Julie and I to go to a concert.

I've arranged for Julie and myself to go to a concert.

Is he trying to impress me? His use of reflexive pronouns doesn't!

Adjective: Giving More Meaning

Details can add a lot of meaning to things we read, write, or say. Adjectives can give details by adding information about nouns or pronouns. Different kinds of adjectives are grouped by the type of work they do in a sentence.

Using adjectives

Most adjectives can be used in several different ways:

- They can be positioned before a noun or pronoun to describe something about it: The **fast** runner passed the others.
- They can be part of the predicate of a sentence: This runner is **fast**.
- They can be used to compare two things: The Ethiopian is **faster** than the Kenyan. These are called comparative adjectives. Words like more and less can also be used with comparative adjectives: The Norwegian runner was **less talented** than the others.
- Some adjectives, called superlatives, are used to show that something is the most or the least: The Ethiopian runner is the **most talented** competitor.

fast   faster   fastest

These comparative adjectives can point out which of the athletes in this race is running the fastest.

Descriptive adjectives

A descriptive adjective can change or add to what we already know about a noun. For example, the descriptive adjectives red and lockable, when added to the sentence The laptop bag has two compartments, enables us to know more about what the bag looks like and its features: The **red** laptop bag has two **lockable** compartments.

A sentence about a photograph like this can be given interest using descriptive adjectives, such as **rugged** peaks, **sparkling** river, and **majestic** pines.

QUICK TIP

Proper adjectives

Some descriptive adjectives are proper adjectives that relate to similar proper nouns. For example, the proper noun Europe can become the proper adjective European, as in **European** fashion is very popular in Japan. Proper adjectives, like proper nouns, ALWAYS start with a capital letter—for example, **American** voters, **Mexican** resorts, and **Sunday** brunch.

Adjectives that limit

Numerical adjectives, such as one, two, three, can be used to give specific information about a noun or a pronoun: **Thirteen** steps take you to the top of the tower. They can also relate to repetition (for example, **double** champion), division (for example, **half** circle), or frequency (for example, **daily** newspaper). These kinds of adjectives are called limiting adjectives.

Combining adjectives

Adjectives can be used together to describe a single noun or pronoun. For example, two adjectives can be used before a noun: A **dirty, blue** hat had been left on the beach. In this sentence, a comma has been put between the two adjectives. Sometimes it is hard to decide if one is needed or not. The best way to figure it out is to think about the two adjectives. Are they being used together, or as two separate descriptions of the hat? If they are two ways of describing the hat, then they need a comma. If the color of the hat is dirty blue, then no comma is needed.

If there are more than two adjectives, then you need to connect the last two with a joining word called a conjunction (see page 40): The woman, **tired, hungry,** and **sad,** sat by the locked wooden door. The conjunction used here is and.

Using adjectives is easy!

Using adjectives in English is simple and easy to get right. Adjectives do not have gender, number, or person, so you don't need to make them agree with the rest of the words in the sentence. A tree, a woman, a poem, a city, or a feeling can all be beautiful.

QUICK TIP

Articles and other determiners as adjectives

Traditionally, many experts about grammar have treated determiners, such as the articles an and the, as adjectives because of the way they are used with nouns or pronouns. Now, many sources—including this book—list these short words, which usually come as the first word in a noun phrase, as a separate part of speech. The chapter on determiners in this book is on pages 38-39.

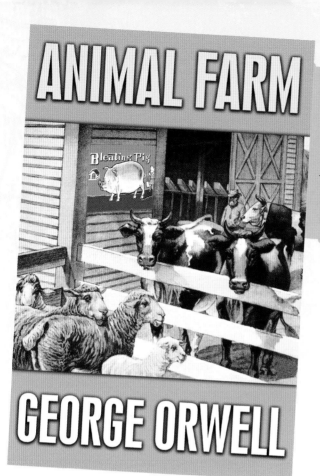

ANIMAL FARM

GEORGE ORWELL

Making the most of description

For a piece of writing to be truly effective, and to make you see or feel what you are reading about, adjectives are needed. Successful writers can really make the pages come to life. These descriptive lines from *Animal Farm* by George Orwell (1903–50) contain many adjectives:

> The **two** cart-horses, Boxer and Clover, came in together, walking very slowly and setting down their **vast, hairy** hoofs with great care lest there should be some **small** animal concealed in the straw. Clover was a **stout, motherly** mare approaching middle life, who had never quite got her figure back after her **fourth** foal. Boxer was an **enormous** beast, almost eighteen hands high, and as strong as any **two ordinary** horses put together.

From *Animal Farm* by George Orwell (Copyright © George Orwell, 1945). Reprinted by permission of Bill Hamilton as the Literary Executor of the Estate of the late Sonia Brownell Orwell

Action or a State of Being

Verbs show the action or state of being of the nouns or pronouns in a sentence. The way a verb is written places the time of the action in the present, the past, or the future. No sentence is complete without a verb. A verb is the only part of speech that can form a sentence on its own—for example, Go!

Active and stative verbs

Most verbs are active, or dynamic, verbs. Some show physical action: Reuben **ran** three miles with the cross country team. Others show mental action: I **thought** I should study more for my science test. There are also verbs that help get across a state of affairs, not an action: I **understand** the terrible grief that follows the death of a pet. They include know, understand, want, and like. These stative verbs are useful at emphasizing how someone feels about something.

WORDS IN ACTION

Physical and mental action

In this extract from *Alice's Adventures in Wonderland* by Lewis Carroll (1832–98), there are active verbs of both kinds:

> Alice thought [mental action] **she might as well wait, as she had nothing else to do, and perhaps after all it might** tell [physical action] **her something worth hearing.**

From *Alice's Adventures in Wonderland* by Lewis Caroll, first published by Macmillan & Co. in 1865.

EAT YOUR WORDS

Transitive verbs need objects

You can't just say I want. What is it that you want? There is a noun and a verb, but the sentence makes no sense. Some verbs, such as want, can only be used if there is an object after the verb to receive the action. These are known as transitive verbs. Add the object to make the sentence I want a new cell phone, and now the meaning is clear. The sentence The baby sleeps makes sense without an object. The action is limited to the relationship between the noun and the verb. Verbs that don't need an object are called intransitive.

Linking verbs

Linking verbs are used to link the subject of a sentence to a word that describes it or renames it in some way—for example, Kamal **is** the winner or Olivia **seems** angry.

This urban scene can be described using many different active verbs—for example, walk, ride, pedal, cycle, and talk.

Auxiliary verbs

Auxiliary, or "helping," verbs help create a mood or opinion: I **must** go or James **can** read. These verbs help the main verb in a sentence express the action or state of being. The three primary auxiliary verbs are be, have, and do. Others are can, may, must, shall, will, and ought.

This chart is a conjugation of the tenses of the verb to be. It shows the changes required of a verb for grammatical purposes. Because be is an auxiliary verb, it is almost always used with another verb. Any verb can be laid out like this:

Conjunction of "to be"

Principle parts

Present	Past	Past participle
be am are is	was were	been

Conjugation

Simple present		Past present	
Singular	**Plural**	**Singular**	**Plural**
1. I am	1. We are	1. I was	1. We were
2. You are	2. You are	2. You were	2. You were
3. He (she, it) is	3. They are	3. He was	3. They were

Simple future (shall, will)

Singular	Plural
1. I shall/will be	1. We shall/will be
2. You will be	2. You will be
3. He (she, it) will be	3. They will be

Present perfect (have, has)		Past perfect (had)	
1. I have been	1. We have been	1. I had been	1. We had been
2. You have been	2. You have been	2. You had been	2. You had been
3. He (she, it) has been	3. They have been	3. He (she, it) had been	3. They had been

Future perfect (shall, will have)

Singular	Plural
1. I shall/will have been	1. We shall/will have been
2. You will have been	2. You will have been
3. He (she, it) will have been	3. They will have been

Lie or lay?

People often make mistakes using the verbs lay or lie. Lay should be used when the meaning relates to the placement of an object. It is a transitive verb and therefore must ALWAYS be used with an object that takes the action of the verb: Jared **lays** the book on the table. The verb lie means to recline. It is an intransitive verb, so it does not need to have an object to receive the action: Jared **lies** down. Remember this, and getting it right will be easy!

To be or not to be, that is the question.

In this famous line from a speech in William Shakespeare's play *Hamlet*, the helping verb be is used on its own. The word living isn't after be in the speech, but you are supposed to figure out that what Hamlet means is To be living or not to be living. The missing words are implied. Another example of this is if you are asked if you can ride a bike, you might only answer Yes, I can, rather than Yes, I can ride.

Regular and irregular verbs

In the past tense, regular, or weak, verbs, always end in -ed, or more rarely -t. This is the most common way verbs show the past—for example, watched, helped, mowed, burned, or played. However, some verbs shift from the present tense to the past tense with a change in spelling or a completely different word. This type of verb is called an irregular, or strong, verb—for example, swim to swam, drink to drank, see to saw, or go to went. Out of all the verbs in English, only about 200 are irregular. See the list on page 50 for those most commonly used.

What exactly are verb tenses?

Tenses are the different forms of a verb that relate to the time when something happens. If something is happening now, you write or speak in the present tense. If it has already happened, you use the past tense. If it hasn't happened yet, but is going to, you use the future tense. Here are some examples using the verb help:

I **help** my teacher. [present]
I **helped** my teacher last week. [past]
I **will help** after school on Monday. [future]

WORDS IN ACTION

Battling verbs

The verbs in a piece of writing help the reader see the action and feel the emotions. This is certainly the case in the following extract, describing a battle to the death with an evil wolf-like creature:

Peter did not feel very brave: indeed, he felt he was going to be sick. But that made no difference to what he had to do. He rushed straight up to the monster and aimed a slash of his sword at its side. That stroke never reached the Wolf. Quick as lightning it turned round, its eyes flaming, and its mouth wide open in a howl of anger. If it had not been so angry that it simply had to howl it would have got him by the throat at once. As it was—though all this happened too quickly for Peter to think at all—he had just time to duck down and plunge his sword, as hard as he could, between the brute's forelegs into its heart.

From *The Lion, the Witch, and the Wardrobe* by C.S. Lewis (1898–1963), copyright © C.S. Lewis Pte. Ltd. 1950. Extract reprinted by permission

Mix and match

Within the different divisions of verbs described on page 28, and often depending on how they are used, verbs can belong to more than one classification. For example, a verb such as walk (I walked miles today) can be active, intransitive, and regular!

Powerful, descriptive verbs are always better than general ones for really saying what you mean. For example, which is better: Jeff went down the road or Jeff skated down the road?

Basic verb tenses in English

Every verb can use 24 tenses—12 in the active voice and 12 in the passive voice (see page 31). This makes getting the correct tense for what you want to say quite difficult. However, you can break down the choices by time (present, past, and future) and by using auxiliary verbs with the main verb. This chart shows you the 24 verb tenses that are available:

The 24 verb tenses shown here cover time and number (singular and plural).

The 24 tenses

		Past	Present	Future
ACTIVE	**Simple tenses**	past	present	future
		past perfect	present perfect	future perfect
		past continuous	present continuous	future perfect continuous
		past perfect continuous	present perfect continuous	future perfect continuous
PASSIVE	**Complex tenses formed with auxiliary verbs**	past	present	future
		past perfect	present perfect	future perfect
		past continuous	present continuous	future continuous
		past perfect continuous	present perfect continuous	future perfect continuous

Some grammar books use the word progressive instead of continous. They are exactly the same.

No future?

In reality, unlike many other languages, verbs in English have no future tense. There are no special verb formations to show that a verb is expressing something yet to happen. However, even though this is the case, it is still possible to write or speak about the future. This is done using an auxiliary verb to help the main verb: I **will** help after school on Monday. Also, time is not always reflected in the tense of a verb. Sometimes there are other words in the sentence that change the time frame. For example, here the present tense doesn't refer to time in the present, but to the future: I hope it snows tomorrow.

Mood, voice, and aspect

To choose the correct verb tense to use when writing or speaking, you also need to think about mood, voice, and aspect.

- Mood: The term mood relates to the intention of the writer or speaker, and it affects the tense of verb used. If the mood is indicative, then the intention is to make a basic factual statement: Julia is dying her hair black. If the mood is subjunctive, it is presented as doubtful, wished for, or imagined: Julia should dye her hair black. If the mood is interrogative, a question is being asked: Is Julia going to dye her hair black? If the mood is imperative, then it is a command: Julia, dye your hair black!
- Voice: There are two voices that show the relationship between the subject and the action in a sentence. The active voice relates to situations where the subject does the action: Snails eat the hosta leaves. In the passive voice, the subject is not doing the action, but is receiving the action: The hosta leaves are eaten by snails.
- Aspect: Aspect relates action to time, such as the completion of an action or the duration of time of an action. For example, the sentence I have handed in my history essay stresses the completion of the action, while I am writing my history essay describes an action that is still in progress, or continuing.

This snail is definitely eating hosta leaves very actively!

Agreement of subject and verb: Person and number

Agreement is the grammatical term that refers to the need for various words in a sentence to use a particular form that agrees with another word or words. Luckily, verbs in English do not have gender, so getting the agreement right between the subjects and verbs in a sentence only relates to person and number.

A verb must always agree with the person being used. Person in grammar covers the three categories of nouns and pronouns: the first person (the one speaking or writing), the second person (the one being written or spoken to), and the third person (the one being written or spoken about). All three persons can be singular or plural. The number must agree with the verb form being used. Here are a few examples showing agreement of subject and verb based on person and number: I am a guitar player [first person, singular]. It is a guitar [third person, singular]. They are guitar players [third person, plural].

QUICK TIP

You: Always plural verb agreement

The second person pronoun you can be singular or plural. Even though this is the case, its agreement with verbs in all tenses is ALWAYS with the plural form of the verb. When you are talking about one person, not more, it is still, for example, You **are** a good guitar player, NEVER You **is** a good guitar player.

EAT YOUR WORDS

Wrong, wrong, wrong!

In both writing and speaking, a verb MUST agree with the person and number of the subject of a sentence or it is grammatically incorrect:

Right: Dan **is** Zoe's younger brother.

Wrong: Dan and Lewis **is** Zoe's younger brothers.

Because the second sentence refers to both brothers, the subject is plural, so the verb form here should be are (the plural form), not is (the singular form).

Verb forms are singular and plural just like noun forms. For example, here, Many books [plural noun] are [plural verb form] in front of the boy. If there were only one, then the sentence would be A book [singular noun] is [singular verb form] in front of the boy.

An adverb is a word that gives us more information about a verb: The artist painted **quickly**. Adverbs can also add information to adjectives: The nurse was **incredibly** kind. Sometimes adverbs are even used to tell us more about other adverbs: The tortoise moves **extremely** slowly.

Adverbs add information about how, when, or where something happens:

- How (adverbs of manner): The old woman answered **quietly**.
- When (adverbs of time): The mayor is visiting **tomorrow**.
- Where (adverbs of place): **Outside**, the child was playing.

Most adverbs that add "how" information end in -ly.

Adverbs of degree

Unlike the how, when, and where adverbs, some adverbs let us know the degree, or extent, to which a quality is present—not just "how," but "how much." Here is an example: Katie spoke very **quickly**. Other common adverbs of degree include absolutely, enormously, far, highly, just, most, nearly, quite, really, and totally.

Many adverbs of time and place can be used to describe this railroad station scene, such as soon, later, tonight, and inside. Can you think of any others?

Like adjectives, adverbs can have comparative and superlative forms. For example, the kites in this photograph can be described as flying high, higher, and highest.

Positioning adverbs: Beginning, middle, or end?

Adverbs that add information to verbs can be placed before the subject of the sentence, between the subject and the verb, or after the verb:

> **Slowly**, the tortoise turned.
> The tortoise **slowly** turned.
> The tortoise turned **slowly**.

If an adverb is adding information about an adjective or another adverb, it is usually positioned in front of that word:

> Brad's zombie costume was **horribly** [adverb] **realistic** [adjective].
> Chloe ate her ice cream **really** [adverb] **quickly** [adverb].

Sometimes an adverb is used to add information to an entire sentence, and then it is placed at the beginning or end: **Obviously**, he was too sick to go to school.

Making adverbs

Many adjectives can be made into adverbs. Most are formed by adding -ly to the adjective, such as quick to quickly and careful to carefully. Adjectives that end in -able or -ible change the final e to a y to become the adverb form of the word, such as horrible to horribly. There are also smaller numbers of adjectives ending in -ic that add -ally when they become adverbs (stoic to stoically), and a few ending in -y that change the -y to -ily to become adverbs (pretty to prettily).

QUICK TIP

Don't be fooled

Not all words ending in -ly are adverbs. Some -ly words are adjectives. For example, words like lonely and friendly can only be used to describe nouns: The **lonely** girl liked the company of the **friendly** ghost.

Prepositions are linking words that show the relationship between words or parts of a sentence: Annie wore a hat **with a pom-pom.** Here, with is the linking word that adds extra information to the sentence. Prepositions come before a noun or pronoun, NEVER in front of a verb. The group of words starting with a preposition and containing the noun or pronoun that provides the extra information is called a prepositional phrase. In the example above, the prepositional phrase is with a pom-pom. There is a list of the most common prepositions on page 51.

WORDS IN ACTION

Prepositions everywhere

Clear, interesting writing that gives the reader lots of information, as in this extract, will always contain prepositional phrases (shown in gray print, prepositions in bold):

> Smoke was coming up from **behind** the store fronts. Past Fuller's Hardware, Second Street went west **on** the prairie **to** a lonely building standing **in** the dead grasses. It had four windows and the sunset was shining **through** them, so there must be even more windows **on** the other side.

From *The Long Winter* by Laura Ingalls Wilder, published by HarperCollins in 1940

QUICK TIP

Verbs as nouns

When a verb is in its -ing form, it can be used as a noun: **Climbing** is a fun sport. This form is called a gerund. Gerunds can be used as a noun in a prepositional phrase, just like other nouns and pronouns: I get the biggest rush from climbing.

Prepositional phrases that describe this picture are: Li has her food **on a red plate,** with the burger **in a bun** and her fork **across** the side.

EAT YOUR WORDS

Dangling prepositions

Having a preposition dangling, or stranded, at the end of a sentence is thought by many experts to be sloppy grammar. There is a story that a young government employee corrected some dangling prepositions in material written by British Prime Minister Winston Churchill (1874-1965). Churchill is said to have written back: "This is something up with which I will not put," using an awkward sentence to make fun of the practice. True or not, the correct sentence seems much more of a mouthful than "This is something I will not put up with."

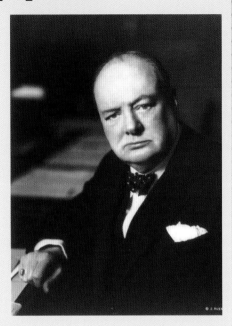

Using prepositions

Prepositions can be divided into two groups, related to how they add information to a sentence:

- Prepositions of place: These prepositions are at the beginning of phrases that relate to where something happens: The mysterious figure ran **behind** the old house. Common prepositions of this type are on, at, in, over, off, under, through, by, into, and behind. These phrases come at the end of sentences. To make sure you are using the correct preposition, think about the place the phrase is referring to. For example, if it is a specific place, at or behind would be a good choice: **at** the crossroad or **behind** the garage. If the phrase relates to a surface where something is placed, then on or under could be used: **on** the kitchen table or **under** the bed. If the place is enclosed, then in or inside are appropriate: **inside** my purse or **in** the school gym.
- Prepositions of time: These prepositions tell the reader or listener when something happened. Phrases like this can be at the beginning or the end of a sentence. Words that can be used as prepositions of time include at, before, by, during, in, on, after, and before. Here is an example of both positions that can be used: Erin should be home **by** midnight or **By** midnight, Erin should be home. Either form is acceptable, but the second example puts more emphasis on the time.

Determiners are members of a word group used individually at the beginning of a noun phrase: **The** math teacher has a crazy dog. Some affect the meaning of the noun. Determiners include articles, quantifiers, and numerals.

Articles: Little words

- Definite article: Definite article is the term used for the word the. It is called "definite" because it implies that the noun being referred to is that particular person or thing. It is only ever used in front of a noun as part of a noun phrase. The can be used with singular nouns or plural nouns: **The** dog barked all night or **The** dogs barked all night.

- Indefinite articles: A and an are indefinite articles used at the beginning of noun phrases. They are called "indefinite" because the nouns they come in front of are not known people or things. A is used in front of nouns that start with a consonant: **A** dog [unknown] barked all night. An is used in front of nouns that start with a vowel: An apple [any eating apple] makes a good snack. The indefinite articles are only ever used with singular nouns. You would never say A taxis were parked outside, because the noun taxis is plural.

QUICK TIP

Exceptions starting with h

Although the letter h is a consonant, sometimes words starting with h are given an as their indefinite article. Some grammar experts say this should only happen if the h is silent (The king needs an heir). Others say it is acceptable to use an as the indefinite article with any noun beginning with h.

When you use noun phrases, such as three athletes or first place, then the numbers are being used as determiners. If you say He has a **nine** on his uniform, then the number is being used as a noun.

With personal names, articles are never used: Jenny and her dog, Fido, are going for a walk. However, these nouns need articles: **The** woman is shown with **the** family dog.

EAT YOUR WORDS

No determiner

You would never say A Sophie went shopping with me or The Tom bought tickets for the concert! Some nouns, even at the beginning of a sentence, do not need a determiner. Examples of these include all personal names, many general plural nouns, and noncount nouns. Words that don't need a determiner are called zero determiners.

Quantifiers: Information about quantity

The determiners known as quantifiers include such words as some and any, which say something about the quantity of the noun. Here is an example: **No** goals were scored in the game. Other quantifiers include all, both, each, enough, every, few, many, most, and several. When they appear before a noun, both cardinal numbers (one, two, three, and so on) and ordinal numbers (first, second, third, and so on) can also add information about quantity.

Conjunction: Making a Connection

Conjunctions are the part of speech used to connect ideas in a sentence. The most common conjunctions are and, but, and or.

Coordinating conjunctions

Coordinating conjunctions are used to connect groups of words of equal importance. For example, in the phrase eggs and bacon, the two words linked by and are of equal status in the phrase. In the longer sentence I love eggs, **but** I don't like bacon, once again the two groups of words connected (by but) are of equal importance to the syntax of the sentence. The most common coordinating conjunctions are and, but, for, nor, or, so, and yet.

Subordinating conjunctions

The phrases connected by a subordinating conjunction are not of equal value in the sentence: Sarah jumped off the bridge on the bungee cord, **although** she was absolutely terrified. The more important part is a main clause and could stand on its own as a sentence: Sarah jumped off the bridge on the bungee cord, and the other is subordinate, or depends on it. A subordinating conjunction usually comes before the subordinate clause. In most cases, it is possible for a subordinating conjunction to come at the beginning of the sentence: **Although** she was absolutely terrified, Sarah jumped off the bridge on the bungee cord. Some common subordinating conjunctions are after, although, as, because, before, since, though, until, when, where, and while.

Here, the subordinating conjunction is the word before: Dex was really scared of heights **before** he bungee-jumped off the bridge.

Correlatives: Two conjunctions working together

You can use a pair of conjunctions together in a sentence to connect, compare, or contrast things. The chart below shows some of the pairs that are used together and examples of how they are used:

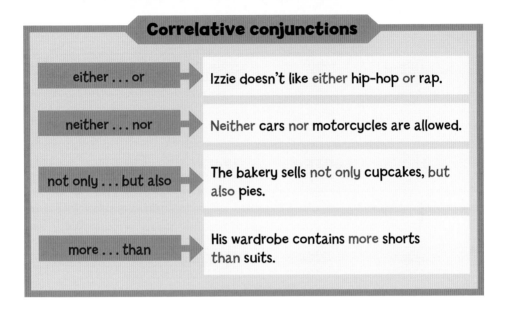

Correlative conjunctions

either . . . or	Izzie doesn't like either hip-hop or rap.
neither . . . nor	Neither cars nor motorcycles are allowed.
not only . . . but also	The bakery sells not only cupcakes, but also pies.
more . . . than	His wardrobe contains more shorts than suits.

Interjection: The WOW! Factor

Interjections are parts of speech that show surprise, emotion, or sounds. They are usually a single word or a short phrase, and they often end in an exclamation mark when written.

Types of interjection

There are many different interjections, but most fit into the five categories below. Some can be used in more than one way:

- Those that express surprise or excitement: These include ah!, eek!, hey!, hooray!, oh!, well!, wow!, and yikes!.
- Those that express pain: These include ah!, oh!, and ouch!.
- Those that express hesitation: Er, hmm, uh, um, and well are common hesitation words. These are sometimes used when a speaker is trying to think what to say next. They are often used when conversations are written as dialogue in a novel or a play, and they have no meaning.
- Those that express grief or sadness: Common words of this type include ah, alas, and dear.
- Those that represent a sound: There are many words that are commonly used to represent certain sounds, such as bang! for a gun shot, bow-wow! for a dog barking, and pow for a fist fight. Sound interjections can also be made up to represent a particular noise, such as "Tweet" the baby bird called loudly for its mother.

BANG!

Making conversations real

Interjections can be very useful in getting across the real spirit of written dialogue and making it lifelike:

> "**Well**, since y'all don't seem to know nothin'," said T. J., in his usual sickening way of nursing a tidbit of information to death, "maybe I ought not to tell y'all. It might hurt y'all's little ears."

> "**Ah**, boy," I said, "don't start that mess again." I didn't like T. J. very much and his stalling around didn't help.

> "**Well**…" T. J. murmured, then grew silent as if considering whether or not he should talk.

From *Roll of Thunder, Hear My Cry* by Mildred D. Taylor (born 1943), first published by Dial Press in 1976

QUICK TIP

Short replies

There are other words or short phrases used as greetings, thanks, apologies, and farewells that are known as formulaic expressions. These include hello, hi, thanks, thank you, sorry, excuse me, pardon, goodbye, bye, and farewell. Words like, yes, yeah, okay, fine, right, and no can also be used on their own.

When people text, tweet, and send e-mails, they often use symbols instead of interjections. These are called emoticons, and they represent an emotional response, just like interjections. Some emoticons can be made using keys on a phone or computer, while some cell phones provide special symbols that can be added to messages.

Using the Parts of Speech

The rules of grammar give different functions to all of the parts of speech you have read about in this book. Some of these rules are straightforward and easy to remember. Others are quite complex and confusing. Unfortunately, English grammar has as many exceptions as it has rules. Why is this? Is it just to make things hard for those who want to learn how to use English correctly?

Blame history

As a language, English grew over the course of centuries, borrowing words and ways of functioning from other languages, in addition to developing its own rules. There was nothing systematic or organized about this process. The first comprehensive dictionaries for the English language were not published until the middle of the 18th century. At this time, attempts were also made to create a standard, accepted grammar for English.

British writer Samuel Johnson (1709–1784, left) created the first comprehensive English dictionary, published in 1755. American Noah Webster (1758–1843, right) was the author of the first major American English dictionary in 1828. It contained over 70,000 words. Webster also wrote spelling and grammar textbooks that educated generations of American schoolchildren. However, nothing was done to try to make the way English had developed fit the new rules. So, all the c. 500 million English speakers in the world are stuck with a language that often breaks its own rules.

The French language is controlled—unlike English, which no one is in charge of!

The English language does not have a governing body that regulates what is acceptable and what is not. However, in France, since 1635, L'Academie Française has handed down decisions about French. The members, known as "immortals," make official pronouncements relating to French and publish official dictionaries. The group tries to make people use French rather than "loan words" from other languages. It even makes up French words to replace the mainly English words that are commonly used (for example, *ordinateur*, for the English word computer).

The official decisions of L'Academie Française are not binding. Many French people use loan words—mainly technical words from English.

EAT YOUR WORDS
No one in charge!

Most of the major languages of the world have a group in charge of setting the standards for the language and accepting changes. This is not the case with English. There is no organization that can make decisions that are accepted by all of the English speakers in the world.

Making it work for you

Knowing that English is full of dangers and pitfalls, just waiting to trick you, makes it even more important to use the parts of speech accurately. Here are a few more ideas about how you can do that:

- Remember that a sentence is always made of a subject (containing a noun or pronoun and words relating to it) and a predicate (containing a verb and the words relating to it): Sports-lover Amber [subject] loves the buzz she gets from snowboarding [predicate].
- Verb tenses must be used correctly in order to place events in the right time frame. This helps get across accurate information in written and spoken communication.
- Agreement is important in building grammatically correct sentences. Verbs need to agree with nouns/pronouns in terms of singular and plural forms: They **are** big movie fans, **NOT** They **is** big movie fans. Plural and singular forms also need to agree when it comes to some determiners and their relationship with nouns/pronouns. In the sentence These CDs are great, there is a plural determiner (These) agreeing with the plural noun (CDs), which in turn is agreeing with the plural verb form (are). Sometimes nouns and pronouns need to agree in terms of gender. For example, if the noun in a sentence is a princess, then the agreeing pronouns are she and her: The princess never wears **her** best tiara when **she** takes a bath.
- When there are a lot of exceptions to a usage rule for a part of speech, try to remember that this is the case, or if it is possible, learn the exceptions. For example, only EIGHT nouns change to their plural form by changing internal vowels, so it is easy to just learn them: dormouse to dormice, foot to feet, goose to geese, louse to lice, mouse to mice, man to men, tooth to teeth, and woman to women.

When in doubt, look it up! Dictionaries are quite literally at your fingertips—in book form, on the Internet, and even as smartphone apps. Even your computer word processor is there to help you with grammar problems. You really don't have any excuse not to get it right!

QUICK TIP

Learn more!

Because the parts of speech and the rules that govern them only have meaning in use, it is really important to get to understand how sentences are built and used. Another book in this series, *Making Better Sentences*, can help you complete the process.

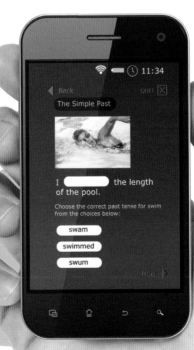

There are lots of grammar, spelling, and punctuation apps available for smartphones. Most of them are very cheap, and some are free!

Using a Dictionary

Dictionaries are reference books that list thousands of words and their meanings in alphabetical order. Good dictionaries can be found as books, online, and as smartphone apps. There are also specialized dictionaries for individual subjects, such as medical dictionaries and art dictionaries. Each full word entry in a dictionary gives the correct spelling of the word, any variant spellings, the pronunciation, and the meanings or usages of the word. It might also include principal verb parts, plurals, and related words in the same word family. Sometimes information about the history of the word is provided. All of the abbreviations and pronunciation symbols used, and an explanation of how the entries are set out, is given at the beginning of the dictionary.

Here's a dictionary entry for the word photograph:

pronunciation and any alternate pronunciation divided into syllables with accent marks

parts of speech for the entry word

entry word

verb endings

transitive verb form word meaning

sentence showing usage of meaning

photograph (fō´tə gräf´, -graf´) *n.,v.,* **-graphed, -graphing**. *n.***1**. image taken by one of several photographic processes. *vt.* **2**. to take photograph of . *vi.* **3**. to practice photography. **4**. to be photographed or be the subject of a photograph. *The flowers photographed beautifully.* **photographer** *n.* – **photographic** *a.* –**photography** *n.* [*Gk* photo- +-graph 1839]

noun form word meaning

intransitive verb form word meanings

history of word, with language of origin of the parts and date of first use

other words in the same word family that also have entries in the dictionary

Pronouns Chart

Here is a table of pronouns by type:

Pronoun

Personal

I, we
my, mine, our, ours
me, us
you
your, yours
he, she, it, they
his, hers, its
their, theirs
him, her, it, them

Demonstrative

this
these
that
those

Indefinite

all
any
anything
both
each
either
one
everybody
everyone
everything
few
many
more
neither
none
somebody
someone
something

Interrogative

who, whose, whom
which, of which
what, of what

Relative

who, whose, whom
which, of which
that, of that
what, of what

Reflexive, intensive

myself, ourselves
yourself, yourselves
himself, herself, itself, themselves

Numerical

one, two, three, etc.
first, second, third, and so on

Reciprocal

each other
one another

Some Common Irregular Verbs

There are about 200 irregular verbs in English. These verbs do not form their past tense and past participle by adding -ed or -t in the normal way. Here are some of the most commonly used irregular verbs, showing the present, past, and past participle:

Present	Past	Past participle
awake	awoke	awoken
am, are (be)	was, were	been
beat	beat	beaten
become	became	become
begin	began, begun	begun
bet	bet	bet
bite	bit	bit, bitten
blow	blew	blown
break	broke	broke, broken
bring	brought	brought
buy	bought	bought
catch	caught	caught
choose	chose	chosen
dive	dived	dived
do	did	done
draw	drew	drawn
drink	drank	drunk
eat	ate	eaten
fall	fell	fallen
fight	fought	fought
fly	flew	flown
get	got	got
give	gave	given
go	went	gone
have	had	had
hear	heard	heard
know	knew	known
lay	laid	laid
lead	led	led
leave	left	left
lie	lay	lain
lose	lost	lost
make	made	made
pay	paid	paid
ride	rode	ridden
ring	rang	rung
rise	rose	risen
say	said	said

Common Prepositions

This is an alphabetical list of the most commonly recognized prepositions:

Prepositions

aboard	during	per
about	except	regarding
above	excepting	respecting
according to	excluding	round
across	following	save
after	for	since
against	from	through
along	in	throughout
amid (amidst)	inside	till
among (amongst)	in spite of	to
around	instead of	toward
as	into	under
at	like	underneath
before	mid	unlike
behind	midst	until
below	near	up
beneath	notwithstanding	upon
beside	of	via
between	off	with
beyond	on	within
but (meaning except)	on account of	without
by	onto	
concerning	out	
considering	outside	
despite	over	
down	past	
	pending	

abstract noun noun that represents something that has no physical existence and cannot be touched, such as freedom or sadness

active voice verb form used when the subject of the verb is responsible for the action

adjective word used to describe, or modify, a noun or pronoun

adverb word that describes, or modifies, a verb or another adverb

agreement grammatical requirement that the form of a word or a phrase is determined by another word or phrase that it is linked with

article word used to describe the determiners the, a, and an

auxiliary verb, such as a form of be, have, or do, used with another verb. Auxiliaries are also known as "helping" verbs.

cardinal number counting number, such as one, two, three, and so on

collective noun noun that describes a collection or group of people or objects

command type of sentence that issues an instruction

common noun noun that represents something that is physical and can be touched, such as cat

comparative type of adjective or adverb that is made by adding -er or more

compound word word formed by combining two or more other words

conjugation changing of a verb through various forms for grammatical purposes

conjunction word, such as and, or, and but, that joins together words, phrases, or sentences

count noun noun that denotes something that can be counted, such as one dog, two dogs

definite article term used to describe the determiner the

determiner word that limits or modifies a noun and is the first word in a noun phrase

direct object word or group of words that receive the action of a verb

first person person word category that denotes the speaker. The first person pronouns are I, me, we, and us.

future tense verb tense describing a time later than the present

gender relating to male or female

gerund form of a verb used as a noun

grammar rules that deal with the structure of the words and sentences in a language

grammatical relating to grammar

helping verb see auxiliary

imperative type of sentence or mood that is a command or order that something be done

indefinite article term used to describe the determiners a and an

indefinite pronoun pronoun that does not refer to a particular person or thing, such as someone, anybody, and nothing

indicative type of mood of an ordinary statement—for example, My sister is out tonight

indirect object noun or noun phrase in a sentence that identifies the person or thing indirectly affected by the action of the main verb

intensive reflexive extra reflexive pronoun used for emphasis

interjection word used to express an emotion or surprise, such as ouch! or help!

interrogative type of sentence or mood used to describe a question

intransitive verb that can never take a direct object, including arrive and snore

irregular verb verb that does not form its past tense and past participle using -ed or -t

linking verb verb that connects two parts of a sentence and shows a relationship between the two. The English linking verb is be.

mass noun noun that denotes something that cannot be counted or made plural by adding s

modify use of a word or group of words to describe or limit the meaning of another word or group of words

mood in grammar, term that describes the attitude the speaker has about what is being said

noncount noun see mass noun

noun word that names a person, place, thing, feeling, quality, or idea

number in grammar, term that refers to the amount of something. The term singular means only one, while plural means more than one.

object word or group of words that receive the action of the main verb. See also direct object and indirect object.

ordinal number numerical adjectives, such as first, second, third, and so on

part of speech one of the types into which words are divided according to grammatical use

passive voice verb form used when the object receives the action of the verb

past tense verb tense used when describing a time earlier than the present

person term used to refer to the three categories of first person, second person, and third person

plural more than one

predicate part of a sentence made up of the main verb and words related to it

preposition word, such as above, from, and with, that shows the relationship between a noun or pronoun and other words in a sentence

present tense verb tense used to describe what is happening right now

pronoun one of the word types used in place of a noun

proper noun noun that names a particular person, place, or thing

quantifier determiner that refers to quantity, such as many or some

reflexive pronoun pronoun that ends in self or selves

regular verb verb that forms its past tense and past participle with the regular -ed or -t ending

second person person category denoted by the word you, which refers to someone or a group being spoken to or addressed

sentence grammatical unit containing a subject and a predicate

singular no more than one

stative verb verb that describes a particular state of affairs, such as know and understand

strong verb see irregular verb

subject part of a sentence made up of the main noun and the words related to it

subjunctive mood or verb tense that expresses doubt or something that is wished for

superlative adjective or adverb that denotes the highest degree of something—for example, biggest rather than big or bigger

syntax structure of a sentence

tense way in which verbs mark time

third person person category that refers to anyone or anything that is not the speaker or the person being spoken to or addressed

transitive verb that can take a direct object

verb word that expresses the action or state of a noun or pronoun

voice in grammar, term that describes the way nouns are positioned and take the action of verbs. See also active voice and passive voice.

weak verb see regular verb

Find Out More

Books

Aldcock, Donald, and Beth Pulver. *Organizing and Using Information* (Information Literacy Skills). Chicago: Heinemann Library, 2009.

Mack, Jim. *Write for Success* (Life Skills). Chicago: Heinemann Library, 2009.

Muschla, Gary Robert. *Exploring Grammar* (Practice Makes Perfect). New York: McGraw Hill, 2011.

Webster's Student Dictionary and Thesaurus. New York: Reader's Digest, 2007.

Web sites

www.eduplace.com/kids/hme/6_8/grammar
This web site provides quizzes that will test your knowledge of grammar.

www.wordcentral.com
This is Merriam-Webster's site for kids, and it offers a dictionary and lots more.

Help yourself!

There are many ways that you can help yourself improve your knowledge of and skills at using different types of words:

- There are workbooks available for you to use to deepen your understanding of grammar and the parts of speech.
- You can download printable worksheets from the Internet to give you practice at using the different types of words.
- Try to make your own guide to the parts of speech using the information you have learned.